Jeremiah

Speaking for God

Claire Zillwood

Scripture Union 130 City Road London EClV 2NJ

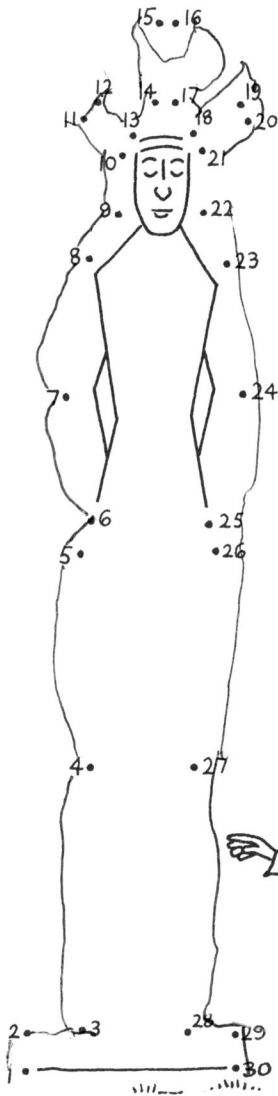

All the Israelites in the land of Judah had stopped obeying God. Instead, they trusted in idols made from stone and wood. God was angry with his people but he still loved them.

God sent a young man called Jeremiah to warn the people to turn back to him.

Jeremiah was afraid to speak but God said, 'Before you were born I chose you to do this. I will be with you and help you.'

The people came to hear Jeremiah at the temple in Jerusalem. But they just laughed at him and did not believe his warnings.

'If you don't obey God,' said Jeremiah, 'he will send a great army from the north to destroy this city and take you prisoners.'

But the people would not listen. 'Our prophets have told us we will have peace,' they said.

Jeremiah was sad when the people wouldn't listen to God's warnings. Sometimes he felt like giving up. But God's words were so strong inside him that he knew he must keep speaking.

Jeremiah watched a potter at work. The pot he was making had gone wrong so he made it into something else.

God said, 'Tell the people they are just like clay in my hands. I can do what I want with them.'

God said to Jeremiah, 'Buy one of the pots. Show my people what will happen to them if they do not listen to me and obey me.'

Jeremiah threw the pot on the ground and it smashed into pieces.

The chief officer in the temple did not like the things Jeremiah said, so he had him beaten and put in prison until the next day.

Jeremiah's friend wrote down many of the warnings. He read them out in the temple for everyone to hear.

Some of the king's officials heard them too, and went to tell the king.

The king
demanded to know
what had been
written. He did not
believe Jeremiah's
warnings either so he
cut up the paper and
burnt it on the fire.
Jeremiah's friend
had to write it all
again.

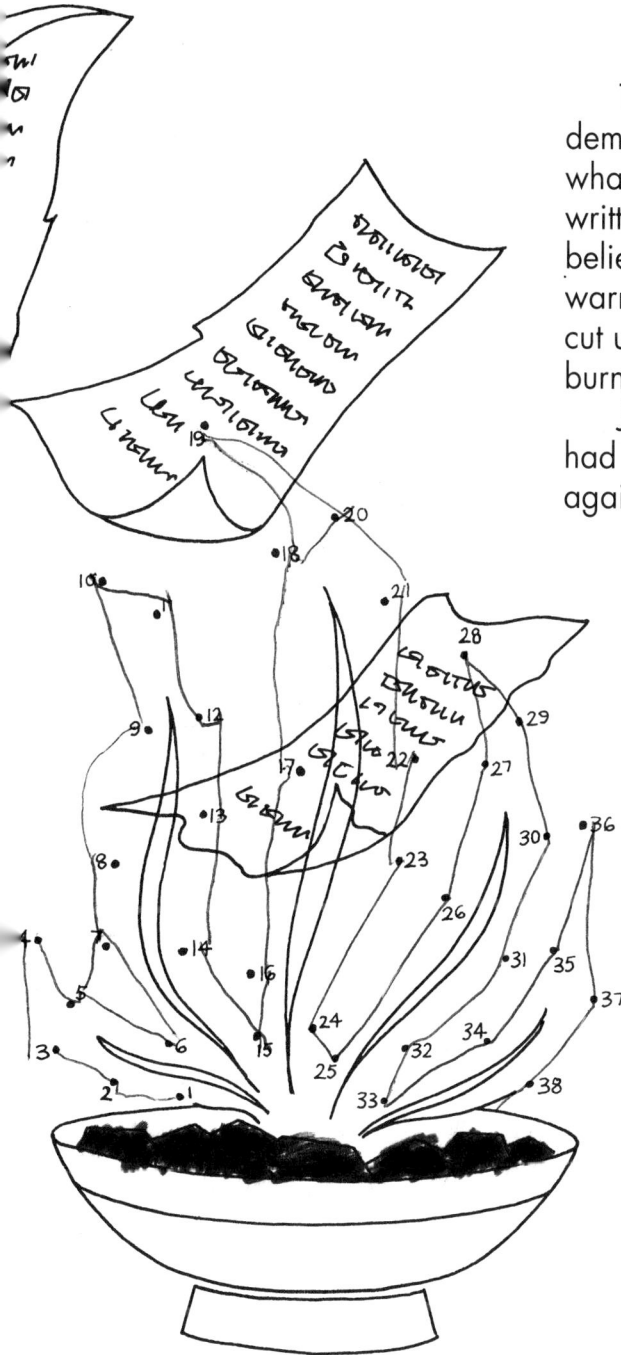

What God had said came true and the great
army from the north attacked Jerusalem. God did
not allow all the city to be destroyed. Only the king
and his officials were taken as prisoners to
Babylon. A new king ruled.

God was giving his people more time to turn
back to him.

One day, Jeremiah saw two baskets. One was filled with good figs, the other with bad figs.

God said, 'The prisoners in Babylon are like these good figs. I will look after them and bring them back to serve me.'

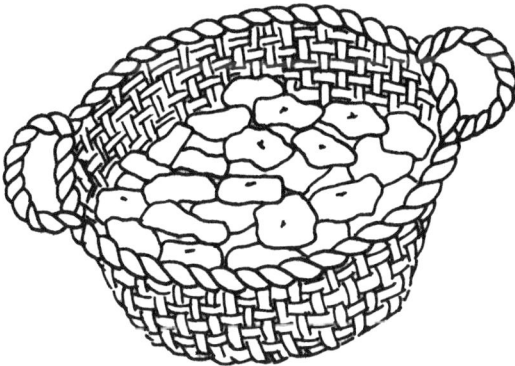

'But the people here are like these bad figs. I will destroy them because they will not listen to me.'

Another day, God said to Jeremiah, 'Wear a yoke of wood on your neck, like an ox, to show the people they must serve their enemies. When the great army attacks again, the people must give themselves up. If they fight back, Jerusalem will be destroyed.'

But the people still would not listen.

The great army from the north began to attack and the people fought back.

'Give yourselves up, 'said Jeremiah, 'and you will be safe in Babylon. And God says one day he will bring you back to this city.'

Some of the king's officials wanted to stop Jeremiah from speaking like this. So they dropped him into a deep, dark well. There was no water in the well, only mud.

One of the officials trusted God and knew that Jeremiah spoke the truth. He also knew that Jeremiah would die in the well.

So he persuaded the king to let him take Jeremiah out of the well and he was kept in the palace courtyard instead.

The great army from the north broke through the walls of Jerusalem. They burned the buildings and took away many prisoners.

Everything happened exactly as God had told Jeremiah.

The enemy treated Jeremiah kindly. They
allowed him to stay in Jerusalem with the very poor
people who were left behind.

Jeremiah continued to speak God's words, but the people still would not listen. They would not do as God told them.

They decided to go to Egypt and they made Jeremiah go with them.

Jeremiah was an old man when he went to Egypt. But he knew that one day the people would go back to Jerusalem and rebuild the city.

He knew it would happen because God had said it would.